Syria

Perry Pierik

Syria

And Damascus' Jackals

Aspekt Publishers

And Damascus' Jackals

© 2014 Aspekt Publishers
© Perry Pierik
© Lens young Dimashqi – http://dimashqilens.com/ar (photographs).

Amersfoortsestraat 27, 3769 AD Soesterberg, Nederland
info@uitgeverijaspekt.nl - http://www.uitgeverijaspekt.nl

Second print: September 2014

Cover: Mark Heuveling
Interlining: Maarten Bakker
Translated by: Ellen van den Broek
Photographer: Lens Young Dimashqi (عدسة باش دمشقي), Lens Young Homsi (عدسة باش حمصي), Lens Young Ghoutani (عدسة باش غوطاني)

ISBN: 9789461536389
NUR: 680/600

All rights reserved. No part of these pages, either text or image may be used for any purpose other than personal use. Therefore, reproduction, modification, storage in a retrieval system or retransmission, in any form or by any means, electronic, mechanical or otherwise, for reasons other than personal use, is strictly prohibited without prior written permission.

Moscow Calling – the West Remains Deaf

Early 2013 no one seemed to care about the political fate of Syria's most powerful man, Bashar al-Assad. By then the softly expressive dictator with crossed hands and a remarkable long neck, looked most like a beast of prey. The Arabic world had been shaken up by the Arab spring and it would only be a matter of time before Damascus' final jackals would have to pack their bags. There was even some speculation stating the Assad family had already left the country. His wife, Asma al-Assad, would be somewhere safe with their children. There were also rumors stating the battle against the Syrian rebels was fought on a ship close to shore. Assad would no longer be able to trust his companions and reinforcements in Damascus. The ship would be anchored under the Russian flag. However, at least the idea had been established that only Vladimir Putin's ambitions for the Middle-East were what kept Assad going. Going against the entire West and the rest of the world Putin stated to support Assad's regime. According to the Kremlin, the world had made a massive error of judgment. Although it was true that Assad wasn't innocent, Moscow believed the alternative would only deteriorate the current situation.

There had been no reasonable alternative to Damascus' regime, and because of personal experiences in Afghanistan, Chechnya, and limited riots at Dagestan and Uzbekistan, in addition to other regional conflicts, Putin warned for the rise of a dangerous political Islam which would continue to disrupt the region. The West chose to ignore Moscow's arguments for a considerable amount of time. Why would anyone listen to Putin, someone who, after all, wasn't innocent either with regards to human rights, and was also a fierce ruler. A series of lingering irritations between the West and Moscow had made sure no one was eager to listen to what the latter had to say. The alliance between the regime and one of the West's bigger enemies, Iran, also played an important role. The theocracy of Tehran supported Assad's regime, although an alliance had been brought forward out of consideration that 'the enemy of my enemy is always my friend'. However, over the course of time Tehran and Damascus gradually became sentenced to one another, and as a result, Hezbollah-warriors from Lebanon, who were Iranian allies, fought on the side of the regime. Aside from the common power politics and economic interests, religion played a significant role. The rise of radical Islamism of Sunni heritage had strengthened Shiite forces. Via Bagdad, where the regime consisted of Shiites, this branch ran via Teheran to Damascus, after which it continued to the Christian and Alavi militias in Lebanon. The Assad's were of Alavi heritage and heavily relied upon this minority in their country.

The Assad family before 1994. In front: Hafez al-Assad and his wife Anisa Makhlouf. In the back, from left to right: Maher, Bashar, Basil, Majid, and Bushra al-Assad

The Advance of the Political Islam

After long fights it became evident that the so-called moderate Sunni forces were no match to the radical allies of Al-Qaeda troops. Finally the West gradually began to understand that Putin's arguments were perhaps not as senseless after all. The islamization of Syria was indeed a threat, and would not serve Western interests. The final straw was the plundering of depots that belonged to the somewhat moderate free Syrian army, by radical groups, after which Western supplies and emergency relief fell into the hands of Jihad warriors. It was unbearable to Washington that as of now, Al-Qaedan messages were written on laptops financed by the American tax payer. What people did not realize was the fact that this had been going on for years. Immediately Al-Qaeda's power base in Afghanistan had been partly financed by the United States after its establishment. This is a recognizable pattern in the region. Based on Israeli financial support the HAMAS had grown. Originally meant to be the cause of discord in the Palestinian world, and opposing force against the PLO, HAMAS grew out to be a dangerous vehicle against Israel. The personal internal logic of intelligence services had instigated these remarkable political maneuvers.

However, the West had changed its mind. Assad, in spite of torture practices, corruption, abuse of power, and even gas attacks, had become a more acceptable interlocutor to the West. What was lacking, however, was the West's vision. To future historians it will be very difficult to ultimately understand Obama's plan for the Middle-East. It remains remarkable that after the fiasco of the Bush government, Washington happily intensified the war in Afghanistan. Overall the costs ran up to astronomical heights. The political gain was extremely insecure. It was and still is difficult to work with 'allies' who can't admit to their own constituency that they depend on protection from the West. The electorate's hatred and suspicion against the West continued to grow. In Iraq and Afghanistan the local population turned out to be adamant, and people were incapable of accepting the possibilities the Western intervention offered. Washington remained stuck between an unwilling population and an unreliable political management, who similarly were stuck between a rock and a hard place. Perhaps the entire situation is most comparable to the situation in Saudi Arabia.

The West and especially the United States, and Saudi Arabia's royal family, share many interests. However, in most cases they exclude each other. This was manifested at the situation concerning the Iranian atomic program and Israel's role in the matter. Officially the royal family of Riyadh complained about Israel's nuclear power, however, offstage they asked for protection from both Israel and the United States against the rising atomic power of Iran and the Shiites. Because if there is one thing the Sunnites hate more than the West, it's the Shiites. All this reminds one of a scenario from the thirty year war (religion) in Europe. During this war turmoil went hand in hand with deeply religious sentiments and humanitarian dramas. At the time it was the plague, now one is forced to deal with refugee issues and all the consequences it entails.

The United States secretly supplied weapons and training to Syrian rebels since 2012. A Syrian rebel carrying a TOW anti-tank missile

Assad Stands Firm

The result of the fragmented resistance against Assad, the retreating Western help, and the unbreakable allegiance of Moscow and Tehran to Bashar al-Assad, was that the regime in Damascus is still in charge. Although the country is heavily fragmented, the regime is still of importance to Syria, and has, since the second half of 2013, been successful. Assad's militias and troops, allies of Iranian sympathizers and mafia-clans, were successful in ending the rebels, the impetuous march. Amongst the rebels fights have erupted as well, where other parties, the Kurds, for instance, also began to interfere. Quite recently, in April, the president of the Kurdish autonomous region in Iraq, Massoud Barzani, was interviewed, during which he stated that they were prepared to deal with the extremists, even outside their own region borders. He clearly brought forward the interests of 'Kurdistan'. The safety of the Kurds was priority number one.

One who knows that the Kurds live scattered throughout the region, and who are also victims of Assad and the Jihad warriors, knows how far-fetched these statements are and how close we are to a supra-regional conflict. 'We will not hesitate to strike', he stated. Aside from these problems, the West struggles with other matters. Not only do they face crisis hotspots such as Mali and the Central-African republic, in addition to the islamization of the Sahel, they also have to deal with young Muslims who move towards Syria to fight amongst the Jihad warriors. Upon return these young-adults run the risk of getting out of control. Radical Jihad websites have the effect of drawing people in. The Netherlands and Belgium are also forced to deal with this problem. In the Flemish and Dutch press, reports on Flemish and Dutch Jihad warriors who have moved to Syria, are often printed. According to Flemish media sources, based on reports of tapped Jihad phones, these citizens are guilty of committing terrible crimes against humanity. In the meantime, news has come forward concerning the suicide bombings of several Dutch Jihad warriors. Governments worry that these war veterans will never be able to integrate in to the West again. Syria hasn't been a regional conflict anymore for quite some time as it affects the region and neighboring countries. More reason to keep a close eye on this civil war with a supra-regional character.

The president of the Syrian Arabic Republic, Bashar al-Assad during a congress

Dutch Jihad warriors who are fighting in Syria would be involved in the horrors

The Death of Hafiz-Assad

At first the expectations were high when Bashar Assad came into power. His father did not have a proper reputation. Covered by the polarity of the Cold War, Hafiz-al-Assad was able to rule over Syria as a dictator. As, in the nineties, his health began to deteriorate, his power slowly began to shift towards his heir, Basil, Hafiz' oldest and most favorite son. However, Basil was into dangerous sports: sports cars. On a foggy morning in 1994, close to the international airfield of Damascus, Basil died in a car crash. His cousin, Hafez Makhlouf, who had joined him that day, survived and only suffered from a head injury. After the accident, big consternation broke out in Damascus. Basil had been trained to deal with the power struggles of international politics and especially national politics, because the Assad family also governed their political and military interests as a family business. Basil had completed his military training with great obedience, and was his father's favorite. His tragic death brought forward a new man: the tall, somewhat quiet, college student from England, Bashar al-Assad.

This was a revolutionary development. Bashar had steered clear from the public eye his entire life; he had focused all his attention on ophthalmology and had become an ophthalmologist. His quiet life at the Western Eye Hospital in London was immediately over. His family called for to him; family had always been top priority, and solidarity a virtue. There was simply no choice in the matter. Damascus called Bashar back, and he came. Of course the young man had to become acquainted with the military regime first. His life radically changed. In 1994, Bashar, at 29 years of age, entered the military apparatus and a prosperous career followed. Within a year he became a major and at the time his father passed, in 2000, Bashar had become a lieutenant and field marshal.

The death of his father turned out to be another turning point in Bashar's life. The old Hafez al-Assad was a sly fox who had kept his empire together via family ties, corruption, and an iron regime. Another private matter turned out to be life changing and important. Assad married Asma, who was born in England, came from a well-off family, and worked at an investment bank. She would remain a pillar in his life as she concerned herself with the regime's initiation of NGO's, in support of its humane face.

Basil al-Assad in uniform

A portrait of Hafez al-Assad from 1996

'The Hope' into Power

Bashar Assad's coming into power was similar to his father's. His father had been chosen as president with 99% of the votes, Bashar received 97, 29% of the votes. This kind of result reminds one most of the communist regime in Eastern-Europe which, in its own way, also 'democratically' protected itself in history. In reality it had already been a done deal. However, new was the fact that although Bashar had been drilled to the military regime, he also adopted enlightened Western ideas from London. It had not escaped his attention that the regime and especially Syria's economy had come to a standstill through incompetence and corruption. Market mechanisms were even nonexistent. In his first speech he stated that things did not have to be like that. The speech, given on July 17, 2000 made a huge impact on the country. Bashar's ideas were revolutionary, and comparable to the situation in the Soviet-Union when people dealt with 'father Stalin'. Although Bashar did not place human rights issues on his agenda, he dealt with the remarkable quality of the Syrian state: the state bureaucracy. This bureaucracy would be an obstacle to the country's development. It was stating the obvious. Additionally, Assad had found a cure to this 'disease', his modern friends at the Syrian Computer Society. The young Assad, at the time 24 years old, would lead Syria into the modern age.

The world was flabbergasted. The Middle-East wasn't used to all these enlightened viewpoints. We have to realize that this originated from the offices of a complete dictatorship and that the world had never before heard the terms Arab Spring. Assad did change the course of history. His nickname unexpectedly became 'the Hope'. Idealistic and optimistic Assad began building what would turn out to be the new Syria. The gap between London and Damascus would have to be closed overnight. Yes we can!

'The Hope' into Power

The Syrian president Bashar al-Assad delivers a speech to the Damascus University in Syria, June 2011

A Faustian Dilemma

However, soon it became evident that Assad was dealing with a very complicated situation. The structure of society was severely anchored. Syria-expert David W. Lesch emphasized that Syria was a typical 'mukhabarat state', a state where security services and the army are deployed to protect the privileged elite. Not least against internal opponents, although the external (Israel – the West) opponents were met with major force. The new young technicians who had to do the ground-breaking work were all young men from well-off families, or in other terms, families who were part of the ruling class. These families had nothing to gain with freedom, as it would only lead to more risks. If Assad's Computer Club would pull through, it would endanger the personal position of power. The grand announcement of the reformations met the robust practice of Damascus, where corruption and loyalty were more important than talent and freedom. Lesch appropriately spoke of a 'Faustian dilemma'.

Syria

A Syrian army tank, T-72AV at Rif Dimashq, September 2012

Overlapping Security Services

Syria is a Kafkaesque maze. Typical were the overlapping security services. In that sense Syria was an exact replica of the former Soviet-Union, or of Nazi-Germany, where the SD, SS, police, 'Gestapo', Grenzpolizei, 'Grüne Polizei', and who knows who else operated side by side. Hitler was very pragmatic at this. If anyone complained about overlapping power areas, he offered this person a personal mandate. If, subsequently a competitor came, he was given the same mandate as well. With this divide and conquer strategy Hitler kept all strings in hand. In Syria these strings were held in the offices of the Assad family, and no computer generation was able to cut them just like that. Syria's population was relatively poor. Low and middle incomes dominated society. The private sector was controlled by family clans and the governmental jobs were based on a clientele system and just as rotten as the ones in the former Eastern bloc countries.

Syria

Employees were simply not chosen based on skills but on loyalty. Corruption was how one earned additional money. The country earned its money with the export of oil, however, they did so on a smaller scale than neighboring countries, and with agricultural products. Assad felt forced to change his well-intended plans for reform, after the establishment on which his regime leaned told him to back down. The days of Assad's 'hope' turned out to be a youthful sin. His security services washed the illusions away with the blood of the reformists, who had made use of the opportunities.

The End of the 'Damascus Spring' and the Muslim Brotherhood

The 'Damascus Spring' had come to an end. The regime turned in on itself more than ever. In addition, because of the slow fading of the Cold War, people began to feel like they were on their own. It was difficult wanting to be important in the world or society, because who would want to invest in a country without a considerable amount of raw materials, with a non-functioning government, an infantile bank system, a dominant black market, and build-in ethnic-religious instability?

The latter had already left a trail of blood throughout the country. In 1982, long before Bashar Assad came into power, his father's old regime had dealt with the Muslin brotherhood in the city of Hama. The conflict between the Muslim brotherhood and the Assad regime was in many ways a precursor to the current conflict. The Assad's in Syria originated from an Alavi family, and especially the army relied on the Alavi population. The Muslim brotherhood in Syria relied upon the Sunni creed. The Muslim brotherhood, also known as 'the brotherhood', never pretended to keep their political agenda hidden. This wasn't the clientele system of the Assad family, with its relatively modern alevistic ideas, but distinguished itself with an adamant obedience to Allah and his prophet. To summarize: 'Allah is our goal, the Koran our constitution, the prophet our leader, strife is our road, and to die for Allah our aspiration'.

The Muslim Brotherhood's logo

War against the Muslim Brotherhood

The brotherhood's loyalty lay with old-Islamic roots. The brotherhood was of Egyptian decent, established in 1928 in response to the growing contacts with the West, and extremely reactionary. People fought for the preservation of the Islamic culture and desired an Islamic state, one cleansed of Western influence.

Their desires directly opposed the interests of the Assad family, in addition to the interests of other rulers in the Middle-East and Egypt. There, after a failed attempt to kill Nasser, the brotherhood was forcefully dealt with in 1953. The 'brothers', at that time under the command of Hasan al-Hodeibi, were banned by the government of Cairo and their leader was condemned to death and executed. However, this never led to the complete disappearance of the brotherhood in the political scene. The current tensions in Egypt, after the fall of president Morsi, are to a certain extent still connected to the brotherhood.

In 1982 the views of Assad's Ba'ath-party, which were in fact linked to Arabic 'socialism' – although the word 'socialism' was often inappropriately used – directly opposed the brotherhood's worldview. The first big test of strength occurred in 1979 in Aleppo, which is currently involved in the conflict. In 1982 Damascus fought back at the city of Hama, where a tremendous bloodbath was caused amongst the Muslim brothers. These massacres, who by some have been characterized as a 'genocide of the Sunnites', became world news after the release of a report written by journalist Robert Fisk, who witnessed the fights. Estimates assumed that there were approximately 20.000 people who died. However, others believed the number to be 25.000 (Amnesty International), up to 48.0000 (opponents to the regime). The British power politics of the Ba'athregime worked. The Muslim brothers kept a low profile until the Arab Spring gave them wings and the politic Islam and the Jihad had returned to the Syrian arena.

The Regime's Isolation

After the Arab Spring had taken a hold on the region, the world, and to the Middle-East, rapidly began to change. Old and familiar values were at once not so certain anymore. After its commencement in Tunisia the 'spring' permeated through the Arabic world. In the meantime it had become evident that the developments the spring brought forward, were not always based on enlightened ideas. According to Western values, Tunisia is perhaps the most successful with regards to Western values, although Islamite's have tried to block the 'open society', and radical Muslims, including the butcher in his bloody uniform with his butcher's knife, have tried to claim their influence at local TV-stations. To the West there were several important side-effects such as the fall of Mohammed Khadafy. However, the country's division caused by tribal gangs after his fall, can hardly be called an example of progress. In addition, similar to Assad, Khadafy understood the dangers of the rising Jihad warriors. As a result Khadafy had offered his support against the radicals. Assad had also set himself up as a figure head against the evils of Al-Qaeda in 2013.

However, before Assad put himself in that position, the isolation of the regime had become a major safety risk. In fact, since the end of the Cold War, Damascus began to see itself surrounded by enemies. Israel was feared, not only on an ideological, but also on a military scale. In addition, Israel was prepared to use its armored fist if necessary. The invasion of Lebanon in 1982 and 1983 exemplifies this most. However, even afterwards Israel would struck if one deemed it necessary. In 2003 the American invasion of Iraq commenced, after which a new and Western oriented regime was established at the Syrian border. The military force of the Americans turned out to be overwhelming. The Iraqi army, on paper one of the largest armies in the world, had been annihilated. Because afterwards the implementation of a civil society completely failed, Iraq remained an unstable neighboring country, which Syria treated ambiguously.

For instance, the chaos could lead to the transfer of Jihad warriors. On the other hand people feared the 'Western model state', which would try to change the Syrian regime. The result was Syria's involvement in the phony war against the pro-Western regime, which, according to the United States and Israel, should be considered a 'terrorism supporting regime', which, after

9/11, was a situation of isolation, intimidation, and boycott. In addition, there were multiple signs stating Syria was involved in state terrorism. Especially in Lebanon, Syria interfered and got rid of political opponents. These events are tied to the Hezbollah, Iranian battle militias, who threatened the southern border of Israel, and who, during Assad's lingering conflict, became a significant ally. The cooperation with the Hezbollah meant the unification of Iran and Tehran.

Moammar Mohammed al-Qadhaf

Assad and Ahmadinejad

The West responded in a state of shock to the so-called 2006 country Report on Lebanon, where amongst other things, the murder of the Lebanese premier Rafik Hariri was discussed. When Hezbollah entered the stage, the accusations weren't only made against Syria, which closely cooperated with them, but also against Tehran, where the theocratic regime of Mahmoud Ahmadinejad reigned. In addition to the United States and the United Kingdom, which responded to Assad' allegations, France, which had always been involved in matters concerning Lebanon, responded to the Hariri case. The Lebanese president was a confidant and personal friend of Jacques Chirac, the president of France, who as a result, stated to be extremely upset about the brute assassination.

Distinct interest agreements between Assad and Ahmadinejad existed. Both regimes were on the Muslim Brotherhood's death list, who considered them to be apostates and traitors of true religion. Additionally both regimes were at odds with the West. It had been a dragging conflict, which commenced with the occupation of the American embassy under the command of Kmoheini. In addition, under the command of Mohammed Khatami the relation with the West barely improved. The rise of Ahmadinejad even deteriorated the relationship. Born in 1956, Mahmoud Ahmadinejad is known for his fierce anti-Western and anti-Jewish attitude. His beliefs and anti-Semitism go as a far as him denying the Holocaust, although these statements were later on partly revoked. The fact remains that his relationship with Israel and Judaism is extremely complicated. In Tehran it is even stated that Ahmadinejad's cause for his anti-Semitism is very particularistic, as he is also known as 'Dabahhian', which means 'master of paint'.

As a result, in the British Daily Telegraph a discussion arose questioning if Ahmadinejad might have been Jewish, partly because the family name 'Sabourjian' surfaced, which would mean 'weaver of Sabiour', which in Persian prayers is known as a Jewish name. Such matters are in fact irrelevant; in reality it brought forward a fanatical anti-Semitist, and an anti-Zionist which he preaches as religion. It was for a reason that the Palestinian leader Yasser Arafat was welcomed back a hero in Tehran. The support given to the Palestinians by Iran and Hezbollah even gave these parties a certain force of authority in the Islamic world. The rise of the Sunni radicals and the intern-Islamic conflicts that erupted, however, obliterated this appreciation. Ahmadinejad's name also surfaced after the personnel at the American Embassy were held hostage in 1979, and with the murder of a Kurdish leader in Vienna in 1989.

A picture of al-Assad and Ahmadinejad during a meeting between Iran and Syria

Mahmoud Ahmadinejad, the president of the Islamic Republic of Iran

The Green Revolution Fails to Take Place

The revolution was the direct result of the elections of 2009, where Ahmadinejad questionably won from his more moderate adversary Mir-Hossein Mousavi. Afterwards a well-known situation established itself similar to the Arab Spring. Through social networks and mobile phones a part of the youth became involved which led to major riots. It even came to a suicide action at the mausoleum of the former ayatollah Khomeini, the founder of the Islamic revolution. People were distrustful and questioned the amount of votes Ahmadinejad supposedly would have got: 62, 6%. It became a tough fight. However, the regime leaned on the Republican Guard, which fought the rebels off with force. The green revolution (one wore green bands) crumbled as a result of the state violence. A historic opportunity was missed, as the entire Arabic Spring was facing difficult times. However, at this point Tehran and Damascus saw the danger for their regimes. They were undermined from the inside out. Tehran appeared to be successful in bringing down the spirit of the green revolution, during which leadership was lacking. In addition, on a cosmetical scale things changed when the so-called 'council of guards' was established, who once again brought forward the election results of 2009. However, in reality the theocrats were firmly in command. Currently the political role of the former mayor of Tehran, Ahmadinejad, seems to fade, after his presidency ended in August 2013. However, this hasn't led to a political turnover. Tehran and Damascus are still working closely together and cherish the as-Badgad and the positions in Lebanon.

Mousavi amidst the population. June 18, 2009

The Iranian population demonstrates at the embassy of Iran in The Hague

Syria

The Iranian president Hasan Rouhani

The Arab Spring

The regime's hold is enforced by the Arab Spring. As is known the Arab Spring commenced after the death of Mohammed Bouazizi in January 2011. The maltreated fruit salesman had been so disappointed in the regime he lit himself on fire and died two weeks later after suffering excruciating pains. The result of his actions was spontaneous rage, which soon focused on the regime of President Ben Ali of Tunisia, who, on January 13, packed his bags and fled to Saudi-Arabia. The revolution was spreading like wild fire. Here, leaders had also become alienated from their people. The frustrations aimed against the clientele indicated that the 'social contract', to speak in terms of the French revolution, was completely obsolete. After Egypt, Yemen, Bahrain, and Libya quickly followed.

Usually March 15, 2011 is the date used to indicate the start of the riots in Syria, others state January to be the month in which the first incidents took place. In April the army began to mobilize itself against the quickly growing resistance and shortly after a collision took place. At first Assad tried to keep most of his forces out of the conflict by enabling Alevi units to fight. Here lay the basis for Assad's problem. At least 75% of the Syrian population exists of Sunni Muslims. As a result most of them also serve in the Syrian army. The Alevi had a relatively small power base, which represented approximately 12% of the Syrian population. Assad was simply unable to trust most of his units. His fears were justified. Soon after the start of the uprising, and its development into a civil war, many Sunni soldiers deserted the army.

Writings on the Wall at Deraa

Syria-expert David W. Lesch, has pointed out Deraa in the northwest of Syria, as the symbolic starting point to the uprising – or the Arab Spring as people like to call it. This area, with approximately 100.000 inhabitants, was the place where students of a local high school began to write 'gone with the regime' on the walls of their school. The word 'regime' people had to take lightly, especially since there was no real aversion against Bashar Assad himself. In contrast to his father, Hafez al-Assad and his brother Rifaat al-Assad, who struck down the uprising in Hama and carried the name 'the butcher of Hama', or his own playboy-brother Basil, who died, Bashar was considered to be a 'normal' man, without a too extravagant lifestyle. Asma, his wife, was also accepted. A Dutch photographer who was asked to photograph Bashar for, amongst others, the German magazine Der Spiegel, emphasized that Bashar came across as 'a nice man', or more importantly as someone who 'wanted to be liked'. He was the type of leader who immediately tried to comfort a person and interestingly enquired about a person's camera, after which, of course, he stated 'he owned one himself'. In the early days of the Arab Spring it was more about the 'principle' than the man. This, however, quickly changed after the regime bared its teeth and was ready to shed some blood in order to remain in command. Power corrupted.

Deraa had everything to develop into a revolution. Assad's security services instinctively responded to the 'writings on the wall', without realizing they sealed their own fate. The students, inspired by YouTube, were quickly tracked down and arrested. Normally this would lead to responses of apathy. However, now it triggered the consciousness that existing balances of power could be brought up for discussion. Parents took to the streets, people protested. The regime's power, which had always been self-evident, was now challenged. Deraa was, what the Bastille was during the French revolution, the first turning point to the political power relations in Syria. The mukhabarat-state collided with the poverty in the streets of this Sunni bulwark, where many young-adults lived and where unemployment higher than 25% was common. Assad's security services quickly tried to suppress the unrest. Electricity was cut-off, in addition to the water and the telephone. However the genie had sprung from its bottle; in Deraa the uprising commenced, or as

Writings on the Wall at Deraa.

people called it, in Deraa stood the cradle to the revolution in Syria.

Syrian troops heading south to the city of Deraa, where the fighting would commence

The Ramadan-Massacre at Hama-Repeating History

The war had become a reality. Next we will highlight several facets of the war. How did the war develop, which fractions took part, and what were the consequences? Here we will also highlight the colossal refugee problem which resulted from the conflict. Finally we will discuss the responses to the conflict on a global scale and the hesitating approach the West adopted.

Until July 2011, one would label the situation in Syria as riots, a protest with sharp edges. The main focal points being Deraa and Jisrash-Shugur. However, immediately after it went terribly wrong. The city of Hama, where the regime of Assad's father had been extremely active in 1982, had loosened itself of the regime's hold. The world held its breath. This was a real power struggle.

Many Western journalists believed that Assad would be afraid to take action, especially not in Hama which had a rich history filled with genocide. Assad could simply not afford to take the place of Rifaat al-Assad, the butcher of Hama. Shortly after the Washington Post wrote 'Syria's Ramadan Massacre'. Opposite to what many believed, Assad was willing to take action and to spill blood. It was no poor job. Barricades had been raised in the streets. However, Assad enabled his troops to invade the city from four sides. The tanks were shooting point blank at the demonstrators. No respect was given to anything. With aimed shots the minarets of the mosques in town were taken down. It was possible that observers were hiding there, but it was also a signal towards the Sunni community. Snipers were active and shot everything that moved. Again Hama had to be punished and at Ramadan Sunday the fighting began.

The number of casualties increased rapidly, and it was the first time that the West, to the American president Obama, voiced their concerns about what was happening in the streets of Hama. The United States, the UN, in addition to the Arabic League spoke about the horrors of Assad's forceful performance. At the time Obama made one of his many promises: 'In the next few days the United States will increase its pressure on the Syrian regime', he told the world. He also believed that Assad's regime 'had shown its true nature'. On June 17, he repeated this warning and made it more specific. Especially the oil- and gas industry in Syria would be hit by sanctions. However, at the time it were all just words. 'No wonder Mister Assad believes he can massacre the inhabitants of Hama', the Washington Post emphasized cynically.

Rifaat Assad

The Noria's at the edge of the city of Hama

Syrian National Council
المجلس الوطني السوري

The secret was out. This would turn out to be a bloody conflict. The resistance began to organize quickly. 'The Free Syrian Army' was established, an overlapping organization, in which many resistance armies cooperated. In most cases they were divided by ethnic-religious reasons. Here a direct cause of the organization's failure is exposed. In Turkey the so-called 'Syrian National Council' gathered on August 23, who tried to work on a new political course for the country, while everyone counted on the quick fall of the regime. Tunisia still lingered in their minds. However, who examined the SNC up close, got the impression that we were dealing with a Polish discussion without end.

Syrian, Kurdish, Turkmen, socialist, democratic, Islamic, patriotic groups, and others repressed each other. Abdulkarem Agha, for instance, represented the Turkmen, Abdalsalam Alshakiri represented the Syrian Patriotic Movement, Abdulbaset Sieda represented the Kurdish faction, and Tourkmani the independent democrats. There were even women such as Afra Jalabi, who represented one of the many independent groups. Originally she came from Hasaka, but had been living in Canada for quite some time. The Council was thus more than dream, and not deeply anchored in the system right from the start.

Syrian National Council

Abdulbaset Sieda

Afra Jalabi

The Double Strike at Al-Rastan and how it Disappeared from the News

The fights against Assad's army were a process of trial and error. The resistance spread quickly, however, most of the collisions were won by the official army. In Latakia the Syrian navy was also deployed, and the rebels were shot. The most important test of strength during this period was at the city of Al-Rastan. The city with approximately 60.000 inhabitants demonstrated several things. On most occasions, if the regime's army was concentrated, they were able to take down the rebels. After a week of destructive fighting the FSA was driven out of town. However, the rebels were extremely motivated, got a grip on themselves and from Homs a new offensive commenced. In January 2012 both parties met again.

The one thing the regime had feared began to take place. Soldiers deserted and crossed over to the FSA. What was a failure the last time, now turned out to be a success. The city of Al-Rastan was conquered by the FSA (to be precise, the Hamza battalion and the Khaled brigade). One of their commanders, Major Ali Ayyoub, proudly reported that they had vanquished the Syrian army, which was only able to withstand their attacks with some of its units. With his words he struck the nail on the head. From the beginning neither of both parties was strong enough to give the other the definitive blow. Several districts were in the hands of one party, while the other dominated the streets a few miles down the road. Still, the second battle of Al-Rastan, which lasted until February 5, 2012, turned out to be a major success to the FSA. However, what was never really mentioned in the news was the fact that about a week later on February 13, the Syrian army made a counter attack with tanks to try to reconquer the lost areas. During this attack, fights had begun to take place at the areas behind Al-Rastan, at Homs. Here the battle was also characterized as disorderly street fights.

The 'Human Right Watch' stated these fights to be even bloodier. In a short amount of time the rebels lost approximately 700 men, and at Al-Rastan they lost their Jihad commander Muhammead Ahmad. The war began to be perceived as an 'all out' war. The Syrian air force, which was loyal to Assad, released many bombs, which were also the cause of many casualties in Al-Rastan, Homs, and other areas in the country. The civilian population were increasingly victimized during the conflict. The fighting and bombardments continued until summer, including situations in which bombs and rockets made an impact once a minute. At Homs the fights developed into an almost old-fashioned siege, where the defense was starved by the government's army. In February 2014, with the help of the UN, civilians who were stuck between fighting parties, were freed from the city. In May the rebels were forced to surrender Homs. Other cities that dealt with heavy fighting were Deraa (from December 2011), Idlib (which was reconquered by Assad's troops March 14), and Damascus. In Damascus heavy fighting erupted, especially in the suburbs (Harasta). However, in February 2012, governmental troops controlled 70% of the city.

A Syrian jet-fighter commences an air attack on Tel Rafat, a village 23 miles north of Aleppo. August 9, 2012

FSA rebels at Homs 2012

FSA rebels at Homs on May 8, 2014

FSA rebels leave the city of Homs after an agreement has been made between the rebels and Assad's troops. In 2011 Homs was the first major city where protests came into being against President Assad and, as a result, was called 'The capital of the Syrian revolution'. Currently the city is once again controlled by President Assad. Homs, May 8, 2014

Kofi Annan Discussing a Ceasefire in Syria with Bashar Assad

In April – May 2012, the world tried to bring some peace to the cities, or at least reach a cease-fire. However, it was in vain. Because of the war 10.000 people had lost their lives, and the number increased rapidly. Kofi Annan was active in the region and attempted to quieten the arms. 'It will be difficult, but we have to have hope', he believed. Despite an announced cease-fire on April 12, 2012, the parties were unable to quieten the 'trigger happy' troops. Assad's secret services also continued to arrest anyone who acted 'suspicious'. Both parties accused each other. Assad defended his tactics by emphasizing that this war was the result of a 'foreign plot', and that one had to continue fighting as long as 'terroristic groups' were still roaming the country.

At the time both arguments were cast aside by the West, as they still believed a Tunisia construction to be possible. More worrisome, however, was the situation in neighboring countries as the number of fugitives increased rapidly. During Koffi Annan's visit to Damascus, where he spoke to Assad twice, people were fighting at Idlib at the Turkish border. In the meantime 12.500 Syrian refugees had reached Turkey. Annan's peace efforts unfortunately failed. Visibly frustrated he returned to his region and turned in his resignation to the UN on August 2. His attempts to involve Iran in the peace negotiations to create a wider front to reach a solution, had also failed. Both parties believed their military force to be strong enough to win. As a result the war continued, on a constantly moving front from Haffa to Latakia. It was a typically modern war as it was asymmetric. The difference between citizens and militias was unclear. It was impossible for horrible things not to happen, which became of growing concern to the world opinion. UN-observers tried to reach areas from which reports of massacres came. However, as they reached the areas they were sent off by rebels with 'roadblocks'. The war had evolved into a civil war, a 'dirty war', where international law was no longer significant.

Kofi Annan Discussing a Ceasefire in Syria with Bashar Assad

Kofi Annan discussing a ceasefire in Syria with Bashar Assad

A T-72 tank of Russian design used by the Syrian army

War in Damascus and Aleppo

The war also returned to the larger cities in the country: Damascus, Aleppo, and Homs. Especially in Damascus it was a matter of prestige that the government did not lose the fight. Between July and October the violence increased. The highlight was the bomb attack aimed at several confidants of the Assad House. Minister of Defense Dawoud Rajiha, the former Minister of Defense Hassan Turkmani, head of intelligence services Hisham Ikhtiyar, and Assad's brother-in-law, General Assef Shwakat, died during these attacks. Never before the regime had been hit as hard as that day in July. At the exact same time the International Red Cross declared the war in Syria to be a civil war. The increasing discord on the side of the rebels became evident when several fractions, the FSA and the Liwa al-Islam, claimed the successful strike.

However, their success didn't translate into success on the streets where the fighting took place. The rebels were gradually banished from the city, over the course of a couple months. Reaching the end of July 2012, Assad's confidants had taken control of most matters. In Aleppo, things did not go as planned for both parties. Aleppo was claimed by Assad as a pro-regime city. However, (small) strikes had emphasized the lack of a homogenous front. In August 2012 it became evident that the rebels were unable to conquer the entire city. Aside from regime ground units, the Syrian air force and helicopters made matters worse for the rebels. The district of Salaheddin, a bulwark to the resistance, was even conquered by Assad's troops. While one party was successful in a specific district, the other was successful elsewhere, for instance, at the city of Maarat al Numan, which is situated between Aleppo and Damascus and was conquered by the rebels. In addition, several border posts fell into the hands of anti-Assad troops. For instance, the post at the border with Iraq and at the area of Ar-Raqqah at the Turkish border. Recently it appears that Assad's troops are winning once again. Symbolical was the takeover of the ancient crusade borough Crac des Chevaliers in March 2014. This borough which originated from the twelfth century is of extremely symbolic value to the religious conflict. Additionally the conquest of the city Yabroud, after a long siege (since 2011!), is characteristic to the forces' changing odds. The city is strategically placed at the Lebanese border, from which the Lebanese-Syrian road can be kept in check. During a joint operation of Hezbollah and Assad's faithful troops, the city was taken mid-March 2014.

In the meantime it had become evident that the Syrian regime was not afraid to use any means necessary to win. Barrels filled with explosives and nails are haphazardly dumped on hostile districts, or entire residential areas which are labelled as 'unreliable', are simply destroyed by bulldozers. Satellite recordings have supplied shocking evidence of these events.

The city of Homs after fights between the government and the opposition.
October 7, 2012

The city of Homs is completely destroyed, what remains is no more than a ruin. May 2014

al-Nusra Appears at the Airport of Taftanaz

During this period of time it gradually became evident to the world that the FSA was only one of the fractions fighting on behalf of the rebels, that other troops began to appear, and that the war quickly became fragmented. In January 2013 unmistakable proof surfaced. Afterwards, after weeks of fighting, the Islamic rebel group al-Nusra, whose power rapidly increased, conquered the airport of Taftanaz, which was dominated by the government. At the same time another peculiar incident took place in Damascus. In Damascus rebels conquered a district, but also met the resistance of the Citizens Front for the liberation of Palestine. These Palestinian rebels remained true to Assad and had to be driven back with violence. Other Palestinian fractions took the rebel's side. It also became evident that Hezbollah increasingly interfered in the conflict and intervened in the war from Lebanon. A life-threatening combustion threatened the region. The SNC and the FSA slowly lost credit as coordinating organizations, especially after the military successes of groups related to the Al-Qaeda, who could count on financial support of Saudi-Arabia, Qatar and other countries, in addition to Jihad warriors across the entire world, including Europe.

An al-Nusra flag

Scud Rockets and Car Bombs

Over the course of 2013 it became increasingly evident that both parties were unable to win. The Assad regime haphazardly shot Scud rockets at rebel bases north of Aleppo. These rockets, however, were not exactly precise and served no tactical purpose. The war in Afghanistan had already established that. Additionally, the rebels chose to use bomb attacks and car bombs, in Damascus, for instance. However, this did not win them the war. The final major successes, which appeared to lead to a breakthrough, such as the conquest of the Jarrah airport, and the conquest of the strategic city of Al Thawrah, at the significant dam which supplied Syria with Hydro-electricity, eventually failed. Horrendous war rhetoric, as used by Abuu Sakker, whose real name is Khaled al Hamad, for instance, who ate the heart and liver of an opponent (an Assad soldier), could not change these odds. The FSA conquered the Al daba base, the army the city of Abel.

In April Hezbollah was successful as it rid the area around al-Sayr of rebels, in addition to several border cities to Lebanon, during which other militias also participated. The months May up to July were characterized by a series of relatively successful counter attacks made against the Assad regime where one often cooperated with Hezbollah. During that period a video tape surfaced on which one could witness how republican guards from Iran fought at the Syrian front. Several Alevi bulwarks, in addition to positions around Aleppo fell in governmental hands once again.

M-600 belonging to the Syrian army, a variant of the Iranian Fateh A-110

Kurds Fighting Against al-Nusra – the Assad Regime Wavers no More

In the meantime interesting developments occurred in the north, where the Kurds had established their own state. Needless to say this pursuit was met rather skeptically by the government of Ankara. After years of problems with the Kurdish PKK, people were not anticipating the further establishment of the Kurdish national ideal. After they had been released from Syria, the Kurds had met the ambitions of al-Nusra and mid-July 2013 fights erupted between both forces at the city of Ras al-Ain. It was the start of month-long fights between Jihad warriors and Kurds, who succeeded in capturing several parts of the Hasakah region. At the beginning of August it was the rebels turn as they carried out a large-scale attack in the region of Latakia, after which they captured the military air force base Managh after a siege of almost one year. In August the first reports came in which spoke of gas attacks made by the Syrian army at the Ghouta region, followed by an attack. The war had lost all its diffidence. The international community expressed their horror concerning the war. In the meantime the war continued, and during the final quarter of 2013 the governmental troops, supported by Hezbollah-units and heavily armed by Moscow, succeeded in oppressing more and more rebels.

Smoke fumes above Babbila. 2014

Sarin Gas

Before we discuss the temporary result of the war in Syria we have to highlight the drama surrounding the gas attacks. Without a doubt anyone can remember the images of hundreds of victims, amongst who were children, who were hit by gas attacks. By now sixteen places have been pointed out where possibly chemical weapons were deployed. Generally speaking Assad's regime is blamed for these attacks. To the American government the images of August 2013 in Ghouta (1400 dead) were also reason to stop the regime. UN investigations pointed out that during the attacks the deadly sarin-gas was used. 'Surface to surface' missiles would have fired these gas grenades. The reports showed it concerned a 'military gas', thus professional material, which was either released by the Syrian army or by the rebels. However, this manner of formulation immediately led to speculations. Moscow tried to protect the regime in Damascus. Obama stuck to his earlier statements, during which he made it clear that using chemical weapons would be taking it a step too far. According to many the regime was responsible for the attacks, however, it has been pointed out that the rebels could also have chemical weapons at its disposal. The accusing finger went to Libya, which would have supplied the weapons. Khadafy's former regime was known for its chemical weapons, and the size of the weapon used, although the Libyan supplies were relatively smaller and more old-fashioned than Syria's supplies.

American prestige and credibility was on the line in the case concerning the chemical weapons. However, it was a complicated situation. As in any war, the truth is always the first victim and although fingers were pointed at Assad, the opposition was willing to use any means necessary to make the other look bad. With it came another problem, the Jihad warriors were marching through Syria and it became evident that the FSA was losing ground to them. This because of major funds from Saudi-Arabia and Qatar who believed this war was a means to bring down the hated Shiites and Alevi's. Saudi-Arabia and Qatar had been on the verge of war for years with Iran and one believed this war to be a 'war on proxis' with the regime in Tehran. Although they were allies to the West, the United States and Europe were facing the continuous support of Saudi-Arabia and Qatar to the Jihad, who after all did not have a pro-Western agenda. One had learned a thing or two from the situation in Afghanistan. To bombard or in any other way intervene would only bring the Jihad closer to victory, something one wanted to avoid at all costs. The Russian persistence in supporting the regime and the other side of the story, which emphasized the 'war on liberation', began to become salonfähig (accepted). More importantly, Putin offered Obama a helping hand. On September 9 Putin brought forward the solution. He stated that Syria would have to dispose of its chemical arsenal under international inspection. Washington thankfully accepted the gesture and hardly 5 days later a deal had been drafted in the Swiss Geneva. This was an unheard-of paragon of international cooperation. Finally Washington and Moscow were looking in the same direction.

While one was working on the implementation of Syria's disarmament, the American or Western intervention was released. To the rebels this was disappointing. The FSA continued to lose strength, the overarching political organization was also subject to erosion and the Jihad grew in strength, and plundered the FSA depots at the end of 2013, where (American) support supplies were stored. To Chancellor Merkel this was proof that they had been right in being retained when it came to delivering supplies and weapons to the rebels. Although

Syria

people abused and stole from the ones who offered help, humanitarian support needed to be provided, as it was a simple human duty.

People leave their city. Syria, Damascus, Babbila

Two destructive tanks placed in front of a mosque at Azaz, Syria. From March 6 up to July 23, many fights were fought between the Free Syrian Army (FSA) and the Syrian government, concerning the control over the city of Azaz, north of Aleppo. In the end the FSA won and stated to have destroyed 17 governmental tanks. Azaz, Syria

A UN inspection for chemical weapons in Syria

A War Without Winners

The war in Syria will continue in 2014 & 2015. One hundred years after the start of the First World War, or Great War, the world has gotten to know a new type of war where chemical gasses are deployed. Although one has put an end to the supply of chemical weapons the conventional war will continue. By now the number of casualties had increased to over 100.000 (some sources even spoke of 130.000 victims) and every day others lose their lives. The refugee problem has also increased rapidly, something we will discuss later on in this book. It is evident that the troops fighting against Assad's army belong to the Jihad and troops led by Abu Mohammed Al-Golani called Jabhat Al-Nusra. As we have discussed Al-Nusra is a group linked to Al-Qaeda. Other significant exponents of the Jihad and Salafists are the group led by the Iraqi Abu Bakr al-Bagdadi, who has moved his network of terror from Iraq to Syria, and Isis, the sacred warriors of the Islamic State in Iraq and Syria, where French, Brits, and Germans serve. The number of French Jihad warriors is estimated at approximately 700 men.

The number of Europeans in Syria is estimated at 1200 men. An additional rising star is Sjaker Waheeb al-Fahdawi, or Aboe Waheeb, who has become the figurehead of Al-Qaeda in Iraq. His nickname 'Nusayri-killer' (Shiite killer) says it all. This 27-year old warrior's main task is to purge the Sunni part of Iraq. Notorious is his video recording of 'Koran riddles', a theological question which, when answered wrong, must be settled with death. Aboe Waheeb was first noticed on the Western radar after the murder on a British engineer called Kenneth Bigsley, and the South-Korean missionary Kim Sun-il. Aboe Waheeb is so radical, even the Al-Qaeda in Afghanistan told him to tone it down several times. The battle in Iraq had already demonstrated that when one acted too cruel, Sunni citizens began to turn on the Jihad warriors and even tried to fight them off. Ayman al-Zawahiri, Al-Qaeda's number one man, had told Isis to deal with the Westerners first after which they could purge among the Muslims. However, Aboe Waheeb ignored his advice. During mutual fights between Jihad warriors, about 1.800 rebels died in January 2014 alone. Aside from Isis, the group called Jaisch al-Muhadschirin had made a name for itself. This group, comprised of only 'foreigners' is under the command of a Chechnya-veteran, Abi Omar al-Tschetschen. All groups are very different from each other. They often fight each other, which fragmentizes the front even more.

The efforts made by the Jihad warriors is part of a long tradition which, according to recent history, dates back to Afghanistan when the Russians were still around. However, also in Syria it had been evident for quite some time that the influence of the Islam was growing. Clergymen were sometimes even seen as 'celebrities', and radio shows where religious advices were given in relation to social and colloquial questions were extremely popular. The response of Assad's regime was very clever, as they trained their own clergymen who preached a-political Islam. This political move, however, could not turn the tide. The Damascus Bureau, a platform of independent Syrian journalists, emphasized that the radical version of the Islam in Syria was also imported by thousands of Syrians who were working in neighboring countries and were exposed to the renaissance of the political Islam. As a result the political Islam was a by-product of the currency and growing poverty in Syria.

During the final months of 2013 Assad still leaned on considerable units of his armed forces who were under the command of Alevi soldiers and officers. Civilian militias were additionally established to protect the (non-Sunni) population, after reports continued to surface stating the atrocities performed by the Jihad warriors. These militias, the co-called Shabiha, are a major, all-be-it weakly trained, force. Aside from these groups,

Nasrallah's Hezbollah-warriors continue to support the regime. No-one knows the exact amount of warriors it concerns. Some sources speak of 3.000 warriors, but there could also be a considerable amount more. Tehran also sent other units, which, until now, had always been unknown.

In the meantime, to make matters even more complicated, the secular Jihad warriors reported to the Syrian front. With their arrival the sectarian war in Syria has entered a new phase. The warriors are secular pan-Arabists, socialists, and liberals who, in their joint hatred against the Islamic Jihad warriors, have taken up their arms against them and, as a result, are fighting with Assad. The group, which operates under the name of the Arabic National Guard (ANG), would have gathered several hundreds of soldiers at the front. The ANG desires Nassar's old ideal, a united Arabic world.

To them, the fights in Syria are of great symbolic meaning, as Syria is the cradle to Arabic secularism. In December 2013, units of the ANG were fighting against troops linked to Al-Qaeda at Kalamoen in West-Syria. Here, four Egyptian volunteers who were fighting for the ANG died. Wadi Haddad, the co-founder of the Marxist-Leninist Civilian front who fought for the liberation of Palestine, was an inspiration to the ANG. Haddad had been a general practitioner, but was involved in several hijackings. He cooperated with the KGB and was enjoying his old life in east-Berlin at the DDR. After his death in 1978 he was buried in Iraq.

Additionally Assad leans on his commercial contacts, mostly Syrian mafia. The regime, which had always been poor in terms of currency, had been dealing in drugs and arms for years. These contacts with the mafia go really deep. In Aleppo some districts are under the command of mafia clans, some even of Sunni-origin, who have a lot to lose when Assad falls. The smuggling routes also form a secret alliance between Assad and the Kurds. The Kurds, who mostly live in diaspora, are part of an international network which could be used to serve this purpose very well. The smuggling routes, as is written down in a voluminous report of the International Crisis Group about the dangers of a 'spillover' during the war, are running via Kurdish contacts in Lebanon and from there it continues by boat to Europe, mostly via Italy and Greece to other places around the world. The Kurdish influence in the drugs scene in Europe is so significant, that in Germany it covers more than half of the supply. They are Kurdish poppy growers who, at the Beeka valley, covered by the Syrian army, cultivate their drug plants.

The money made is used by the regime to enforce their safety policies. The Kurds made this pact unwillingly, as at the same time the Sunni-Kurds were distrusted based on their nationalist ambitions. As long as the Kurds were protected by Assad the union was maintained. As Damascus was forced to reign in, Kurdish separatism rose once again. The PKK, the Kurdish Labor Party of Öcalan, profited from the moves made by both parties. Running from Turkey, Öcalan was welcome in Syria, where the Kurds were deployed to beat Ankara. If Ankara needed to be pleased, a few significant Kurdish players were handed over. It wasn't an enviable position the Kurds were in.

The Kurdish Pact and Turkey's Role

The pact made between the PKK and Ankara in 2013 seemed to take some of the load of off Turkey's back, who suspiciously followed the developments in Syrian Kurdistan. According to some Kurdish sources the traditional Turkish premier Recep Tayyib Erdogan, of the AK party, would be willing to look the other way if the Jihad warriors of al-Nusra and others would help deal with the Kurdish problem in Syria. It will never come to this, however, it is obvious that both parties are far apart. The position of the Kurds brings us to another key player to the Syrian drama: Turkey. From the start Turkey has played a major role during the conflict. Since November 2012 troops of the Free Syrian Army, originating from different fractions who are supported by the West, are trained for war. This training takes place in Jordan and Turkey. Anyone who volunteered was trained to use heavy Russian equipment, as Russian weapons are abundantly available in Syria.

Turkey's involvement does not surprise anyone. It has been known for years that Ankara wants to make its voice heard in the world and the region. European countries have noticed this, during difficult negotiations concerning Turkey's entry to Europe. The Turks have shown themselves to be proud, stubborn, and not very accommodating. Erdogan's tough attitude was supported by a prosperous economic growth, enabling Ankara to feel independent from Europe which was having difficulty dealing with crises as it struggled with Greece and other weak economies. With it Erdogan had a firm political mandate at his disposal. By now the margin owned by Erdogan and his AK-party has become known because of the riots at the Taksim square and at other cities. It is not infinite. In addition, the corruption scandals at the end of 2013 and the discharches that followed in January 2014 at the police and justice department, of all who were against the regime, enforce the image of a very autocratic premier. To what extent Erdogan would bend to the political reality in his country is unclear. Erdogan is a talented man, who is capable of building a firm political organization around himself. However, he is also very vain and suffers from megalomania which became evident after the leaked WikiLeaks –rapports surfaced. Ambassador Eric S. Edelman warned that Erdogan was an 'authoritarian' and a 'loner' who made decisions in 'isolation'. He did not have proper, critical advisers at his disposal. Continuous miscalculations at foreign political fields had made this clear, which, for instance, led to the unnecessary tensions with Europe and Israel. From the embassy offices the American State Department received clear instructions how they could utilize these megalomaniac sides of Erdogan's politics. That this wasn't an easy task became evident after Erdogan collided with Israel, who had formerly been a reliable ally. At a time when Turkey was at odds with most of its neighboring countries, this conflict was a case of bad-timing.

The premier of Turkey, Recep Tayyip Erdoğan. He is also the political leader of the AK-party

The Geo-Political Interests of Ankara and Damascus' Four Seas-Strategy

What are Turkey's geo-political interests in Syria? On a geographical scale Syria 'blocks' the access to the south of Turkey, at least if one assumes that Ankara would rather avoid the precarious Iraq and hostile Iran. Syria's growing instability should also be considered another obstacle to Turkish ambitions to move in southern directions, to the old mandate region of Egypt, as core nation to the Islamic world, and of course Saudi-Arabia as rich oil nation and guardian of sacred cities. Access to the relatively more stable country of Jordan is also closed off by Syria.

Although Syria is not considered to be an 'oil giant', Damascus has set its eyes on part of the equation, and desires to use the country's location. The Syrians have called this the four seas-strategy. This plan contains the ambition to turn Syria into the energy supplier of the region. Because of its central location close to the rich oil states Saudi-Arabia, Iraq, Iran, and the smaller Gulf states, in addition to the location at the waterways (the Mediterranean), and via (future) pipelines through the

Red Sea, Persian Gulf, and even the Caspian Sea (Bakoe), one hopes that one day the port of Banās will grow out to be as large as the port in Rotterdam. Damascus is playing with geo-economical ambitions where one wants to transfer the Black Sea oil and Gas of Nabucco, Tap, the Trans Anatolian Arab Gas, the South Caucasus Pipeline, and Kirkoek- Banās, west into Syria after which it will be sold on the European market.

With it Assad is trying to carefully charm the West, which for 30% of its entire supply depends on Russian gas. The difficult relationship between the West and Putin's regime have caused the feeling of inconvenience to grow concerning this dependent situation. A network via Syria-Turkey-Greece-Bulgaria which leads into Europe could 'rid' one of this problem. The gas can be extracted from the Persian Gulf and flow via Assalouyeh-Bagdad-Damascus into the Mediterranean. The Shiite regime in Tehran, the Shiite regime in Bagdad, and the Alevi regime in Syria, would be able to form a geo-economical-geo-political blockage against the growing Sunni pressure in the region. All this would also improve Syria's financial position.

The Geo-Political Interests of Ankara and Damascus' Four Seas-Strategy

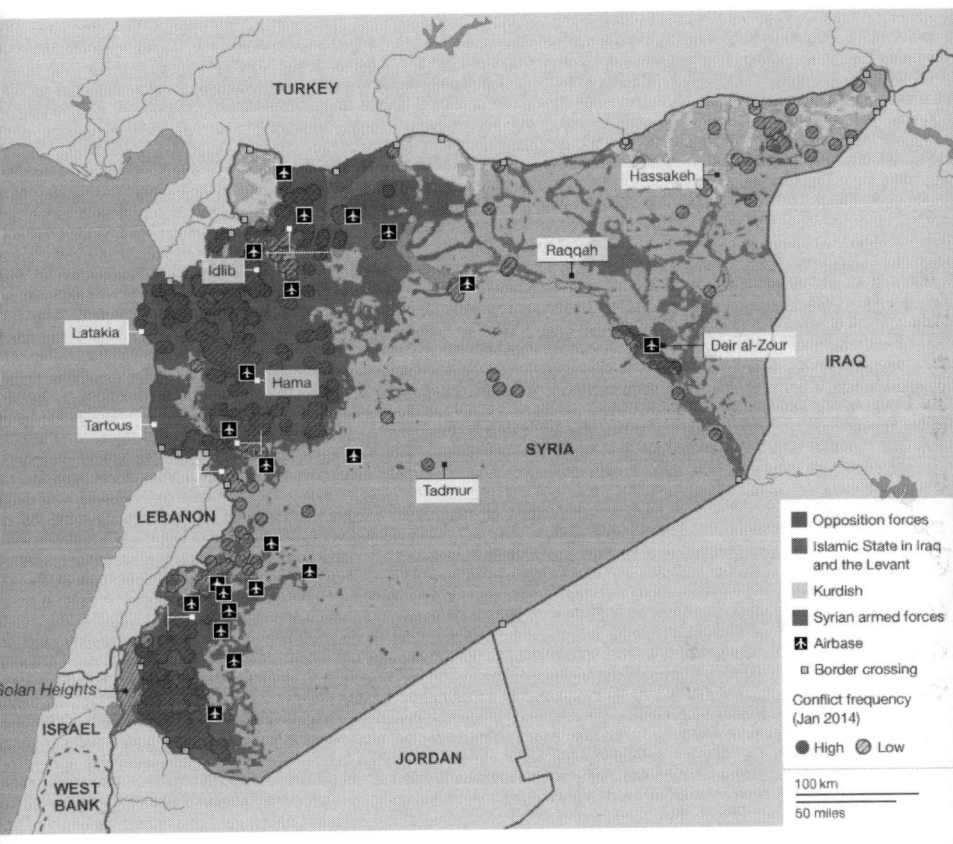

Syria

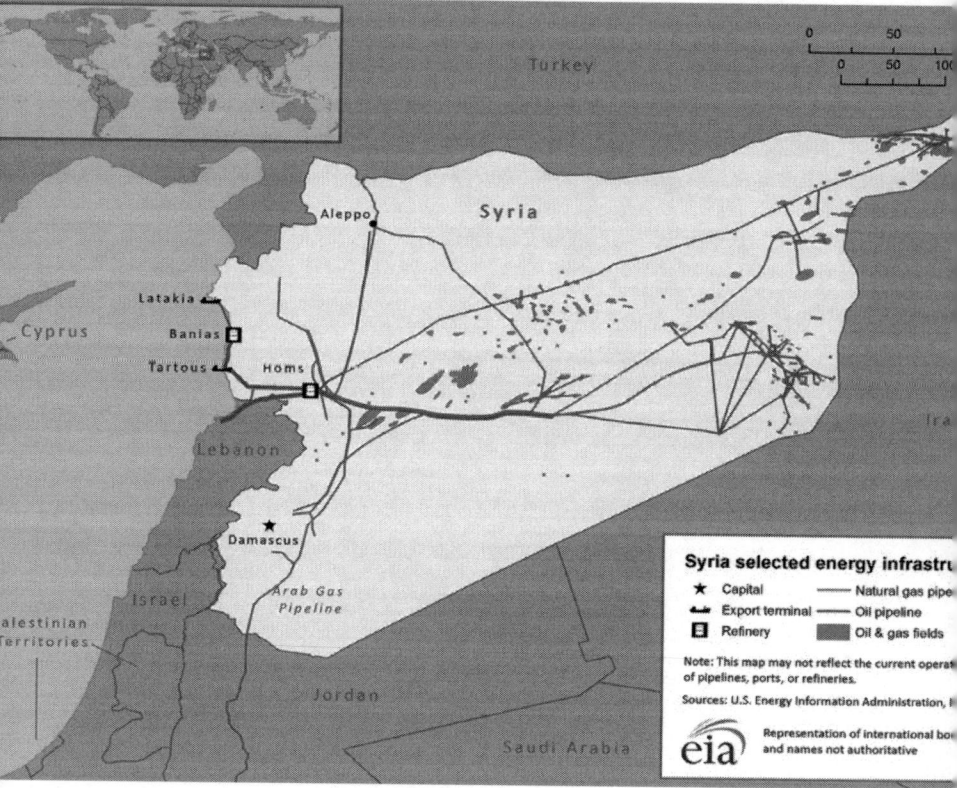

Ergenekon

While Turkey was forced to maintain its position in an extremely restless and dangerous region, the military apparatus had become powerless because of what one called the 'terrorist organization Ergenekon', the internal power struggle which erupted in the country and in which the army plays a significant role. If Putin would decide to use the Russian fleet to seize the power over the Black Sea, the fights against the Turkish navy would become a 'walk over'. The Turkish fleet has dropped back to a level similar to the period in which 'Goeben' and 'Breslau', at the time foreign powers (from Germany), were in command of the Turkish fleet and the provision of vessels. In the summer of 2013, during an almost Borgia-ish game of operetta the high commanders of the Turkish navy ended behind bars. If it wasn't such a serious matter, it might even be comical. First the chief admiral disappeared, followed by Nusret Güner in August. A spicy detail was that he was spied on after someone had placed a hidden camera in his teen daughter's bedroom. Sex tapes are in Erdogan's puritanical Turkey, a usable political exchange. In a country where virginity tests often occur before marriage (also in the Turkish communities in Western-Europe), this doesn't surprise anyone. Güner kicked the bucket and ever since the Turkish fleet aimlessly bobs the waves.

All of this was the result of the 'triumph of democracy', as the members of the Erdogan's AK-party so beautifully put it. The Erdogan government stated to have prevented a coup d'état. Because of it, one out of five generals ended up behind bars, including the chief of staff, Ilker Basbug. This is of major symbolic value. The current Turkish government proves at this point that they do not respect old powers and do not shy away from taking them down. Basbug, now seventy years of age, was believed to be a 'guardian of the secular Islam' which was an exponent of the almost immune corps of officers in the kemalist tradition. Moreover, Basbug brought forward a rational argument against the accusation of 'terrorism against the state'. Why would the army 'turn to terrorism' if one has thousands of soldiers at one's disposal?

Pensioned generals and officers were additionally arrested and ended up in prison. The first major sentences have been brought forward, which resulted into serious riots caused by the opponents. In September 2012, the first 330 officers were brought before court. This purge isn't a one-time event. Throughout the entire country one is purging their nation of criminals. Journalists, doctors, lawyers and politicians are accused of subversive affairs. A Western analyst noticed that all the accused had at least one thing in common: they all had a critical attitude towards the AK party of premier Erdogan.

The Turkish premier Recep Tayyip Erdogan, with Barack Obama. March 2014

İlker Başbuğ

The Turkish Army

Fractured Syria continuously questions Turkey's sense of security, however, their own military position has faded in the last few years. A strange discrepancy is present between the ambitions of Erdogan's Turkey and the army's situation. Erdogan has presented himself as a distinctive leader, and with the Turkish army as additional force within the NATO, he also turned out to be a strong force. The army has got quite the reputation, (re)established in 1949, became a member of NATO in 1952 and was modernized, deployed in Korea, protected the border of Iraq, PKK-operations, amphibious landing on Cyprus (the Turks speak of 'peace operation Cyprus'), a peace mission in Somalia, Afghanistan. Especially to Korea, the Turkish army was the first Western acquaintance. The soldiers with heroic moustaches, came from the eastern mountain regions of Turkey. Their daggers were so long, Western journalists mistakenly described them as 'swords'. Linked to the 8th American army (and in particular the 25th Infantry division), the Turks made a name for themselves on multiple occasions. For instance, at the battle for Kanuri.

Often the losses were considerable, up to a point where 15% of the personnel had been killed and 70% of the material had been destroyed. Overall, approximately 5000 men were permanently stationed in Korea. Turkey had shown some nerve as, second after the United States, it voluntarily sent troops to the Asian peninsula. About 402.000 soldiers currently serve the Turkish army, having at their disposal Leopard tanks, upgraded (M48) Patton tanks and air force troops. The Turkish air force also has somewhat of a famous history. After its establishment in 1911 the Turkish air force was labelled the first in the world, and only one year later they were deployed (with German pilots) during the Balkan war. On the eve of the Second World War, Ankara had American, French and Polish aircrafts at their disposal. After the war they began to focus on American aircrafts. This development rapidly accelerated after they joined the NATO. A formidable force of power? Looks can be deceiving.

Israel's Dilemma

Now that Turkey as a regional power has become powerless, and Erdogan has his hands full with domestic politics, a regional power is lacking who can correct Syria. Israel is not the right country to help out. Besides, the country is wrapped up in a complicated double position. Traditionally Israel and Syria had a tense and complicated relationship and one will definitely not mourn the fall of Assad. However, it is more complicated than that. Similar to the United States, Israel has noticed that the Jihad warriors are a serious problem, and that the conflict against Assad, which in the past few years was similar to the Cold War, did have its benefits. Overall, the main problem was the Hezbollah as extension to Iran, and Israel's fear for the nuclear ambitions of Tehran. Hezbollah has utilized this fear by threatening to include Israel in the war if it would intervene against Assad. Now that Syria's chemical weapons arsenal is dismantled, the necessity seems to have vanished. Across the entire front advances are made between the Shiite troops and the West.

In the meantime the Iranian president Ahmadinejad has left the stage and new opportunities are announcing themselves. The new president of Iran, Hassan Rouhani, had been in charge of the most important geo-political think tank of Tehran for 16 years. In that sense an international apprehension might be expected of him, and camp Assad can use all the diplomatic and political support they can get. As a sign of good will, Rouhani succeeded in preventing the continuous escalation of the feared Iranian nuclear program. Although Israel doesn't trust the clergyman who was born in 1948, most of the tension seems to have vanished for the time being. For some time the thought that the conflict in Syria would be overshadowed by an even bigger conflict between Israel and Iran lived among the citizens. However, for now the crisis is averted now that Iran proved itself to be very accommodating.

Western interventions, whether they would be arranged by the United States, Israel, or Turkey, appear to be unnecessary at this point. With it the war in Syria seems to be on its own, as a smoldering fire that will slowly take down the country. Lebanon is the country most in danger to be dragged down with Syria. The country never really recovered from their own bloody civil war and is built of major ethnic and religious diversity wich makes the country vulnerable.

Busherhr's nuclear power station just outside of the southern city of Bushehr, Iran

The Israeli army defends the Gaza strip with tanks and the armored vehicle division. December 2009

Refugees

Extremely destabilizing is the question concerning the increasing amount of refugees. Approximately hundreds of thousands of refugees can be found in Lebanon, and their position, also because of the cold winter of 2013-2014, isn't very enviable. With their arrival comes the question of safety. A large amount of refugees means tension, mostly because they bring ethnic-religious tensions with them. It is admirable that Turkey is doing whatever it can to shelter hundreds of thousands of refugees. Not much has been reported about Jordan, but many refugees have found shelter there as well. According to the UN Refugié Agentia report, approximately 1.000.669 Syrians were living in neighboring countries in the spring of 2013. About 33% found shelter in Lebanon, 33% in Jordan, 19% in Turkey, 11% in Iraq, and the rest is staying elsewhere. To small Lebanon this means an increase in population of 10%. The Turks have spent about 600 million euros on care and seventeen enormous tented camps in order to provide people with some shelter. However, all of it this doesn't occur without tension. Many Turks at the border with Syria are Alevi and skeptically watch the Sunni refugees. Half of the total amount of refugees are children under the age of 18. The number of asylum applications in Europe, also in the Netherlands, continues to increase.

A young Syrian refugee is standing behind the gate during a protest against President Bashar al-Assad at the Yayladagi refugee camp in the Hatay province at the Turkish-Syrian border. March 2012

The War Will Continue

While the refugees are freezing in the camps, the Assad family clan has put its country houses in the Côte d'Azur up for sale. It would concern about 1 billion euros in real estate. The war, after all, needs to be funded for. For the time being, Damascus' jackals are able to withstand the attacks. They hardly submit their prey, however, they do cooperate with others and share the profits. Their pacts with the Russians, Persians, and Kurds are evidence of this. The opponents are basically the same. Exhausted they are circling each other. Citizens are hiding in neighboring countries and the world hasn't got a clue how to resolve the problem. This war is too complex to be easily solved, which also became evident during the peace negotiations in Montreux in January 2014. The conflict is similar to the Arab Spring, however, it is born with defects, inner contradictions, and is as much conservative as it is stubbornly revolutionary. This war will continue and the world will sit by and watch feeling embarrassed.

However, some things are simply not to be solved, even though they really want to be.

An advertisement for SpeakUp4SyrianChildren at the armored city of Yalda in Syria

Afterword
The Conflict's 'Fallout': IS' 'Blitzkrieg'

The destabilization of the country seems to have enraged the most extreme variant of the Muslim extremist organizations. The Islamic state in Iraq and the Levant (ISIL), also called the Islamic state in Iraq and Syria (ISIS) developed, via IS- Islamic State – and the called for Caliphate under the command of Abu Bakr al-Baghdadi (which is probably not his real name), into a new and feared power force in the region. Via Syria the war was exported to Iraq, where major parts of the west and the middle fell into their hands.

Kalief Ibrahim, as Abu Bakr al-Baghdadi calls himself, has been on Interpol's radar for several years. Formerly active as Bin Laden's man in Iraq, he made a name for himself during the Syrian civil war. Al-Baghdadi was born in 1971 in Samarra, north of Bagdad, and is a mysterious figure. He even spoke to his men wearing a mask, giving him the nickname 'the invisible sheik'. His public performance at the mosque of Nuriddin on July 4, 2014 should be perceived as a growing mark of confidence. Al-Baghdadi's carefulness is without a doubt the result of the death of his predecessor, Al-Zaraqawi, who was killed by the Americans in 2006, and Bin Laden's fate.

In hindsight the fragile Syria, which was easily accessible from Turkey, was the engine behind the growing forces of the international Jihad warriors. Al-Baghdadi could also count on the increasing support of non-Arab Jihad warriors, among which also many Europeans in addition to volunteers from Asia and the Caucasus. Announcing the Caliphate signaled the growing consciousness of power of the radical Jihad warriors, who, with their pick-up trucks, brought forward a real 'Blitzkrieg' in large areas of Syria and Iraq. While Assad's troops were able to withstand the attacks in the heartland of their realm, there where the Alevi warriors and other minorities were stronger, the IS effortlessly beat the corrupt Iraqi army. During the summer of 2014, it brought the IS in front of Bagdad's gates and the young borders of the Kurdish north-Iraq.

In October 2014, the fights began to focus on the border city of Kobani, where Kurdish troops and ISIS were facing each other. As a result, a United States' governed coalition increased the air support above Kobani to aid the

Afterword The Conflict's 'Fallout': IS 'Blitzkrieg'

Abu Bakr al-Baghdadi, the personally acclaimed Kalief Ibrahim

defenses. In Turkey and Europe, Kurdish demonstrators continue to ask for lasting support to serve their interests in the region, where on many occasions the situation escalated.

Afterbirth

As catastrophic as the action of the IS was in the occupied areas – massive numbers of fugitives, mass executions, and misbehavior – the new status quo has created a number of possibilities. For the first time, since the success of IS, new coalitions have been formed which were first deemed impossible. Obama's and the United States' refusal to help the failing Iraqi premier Maliki, because of his one-sided ethnical related politics, eventually contributed to the fact that the politicians in Bagdad became convinced that democracy isn't simply the will of 50% plus one, but that the rights of minorities need to be served, and that in order to create a stable country one needs to listen to what others have to say. The Arabic world, where democracy is an unknown phenomenon, continuously aims towards absolute power even though it increases corruption. The power of the army corresponded. Recent political reformations in Iraq in the summer of 2014 bring forward the hope that a more resolute regime will reign, in order for the Iraqi state to get a stronger position towards the IS and the other problems in the country. From the beginning the Kurds have proved themselves to be a trustworthy partner to the West in the region. However, out of loyalty to the regime in Bagdad little had been done to enforce the pesmerga's of the Kurdish north on a military scale. In reality it was the Kalasjnikov army which would bring the Kurds into the field, enforced with outdated T0-54 and T-55 tanks made by the Soviet Union, and a lost Chinese tank. Thanks to the support of PKK-warriors from Turkey, old veterans who took their arms once again, and arms supplies from the West, the IS' march could be momentarily stopped.

Often feared evil turns the tide. The IS is so radical other parties will have to join forces in order to bring down this revolutionary force. The financiers from Saudi-Arabia additionally seem to be fed up with the extremists. As a result, IS is living in a world with (personally exclaimed) enemies. Nevertheless the region is extremely unstable. Overall, countries as Jordan and Saudi-Arabia are weak. On the other hand, regional forces as Iran and Turkey, and of course Israel, will keep a close eye on the situation. Even Washington cannot afford a lasting instability in the strategic region. The IS' afterbirth could be the sign of new rearrangements in the region, with an independent Kurdish state and a new start for Iraq. However, a successful game of dominos for the IS, cannot completely be excluded. Therefore the region will remain top priority to many chiefs of state.

Works Cited

Aalders, G./Pierik, P., (red.)., Wikileaks. *Tussen cyberoorlog en informatierevolutie. (Soesterberg 2011)*

Abdulrahim, R., *Syrian rebel commander badly hurt in car bombing.* Los Angeles Times 25.03.2013

Ali, N./Addley, E., *At Home with the Assads: Syria's ruthless ruling family. The Dynasty founded on Hafez al-Assad rise from poverty and obscurity is maintained by some uncompromising characters.* The Guardian 11.10.2011

Aneja, A., *From Arab Spring to post-Islamist Summer.* In: The Hindu 12.10.2011

Bennett, D., *The U.S. has been secretly training Syrian Rebels for months.* Reuters 21.07.013

Byman, D., *Why Drones Work.* In: Foreign Affairs Vol. 92 Number 4 july/august 2013

Syria

Callimachi, R., *'Use dolls and statues' among 22 helpful tips ussed by al-Qaeda to avoid U.S. drones*. Financial Post, 13.02.2013

Cleef, W.van., *Rust op Mindanao, voor nu*. Trouw 16.07.2013

Cloud, D.S./Abdulrahim,R., *U.S. training Syrian rebels; White House's stepped up assistance*. Los Angeles Times 21.07.2013

Cronin, A.K., *Why Drones Fail*. In: Foreign Affairs Vol. 92 Number 4 july/august 2013

Dahan, G., *Syrisch strijdperk lokt ook niet-religieuze heethoofden*. Trouw 12.12.2013

Dahan, G., *Meedogenloze twintiger leidt Al-Kaida in Irak*. Trouw 30.01.2014

Dahan, G., *Hoe Isis Al-Kaida is voorbijgestreefd*. Trouw 07.02.2014

Damascus Bureau (journalistiek platform voor onafhankelijke Syrische journalisten) , *A Decade in Power part 3:*

In Grip of Poverty and Religion. Social trends under Bashar al-Assad. 26.07.2010

Eveleens, I., *Geografisch paradijs voor extremisten.* Trouw 20.08.2013

Fisk,R., *Assad, his raid on Lebanon, and Syria's slow slip into civil war.* In: The Independent 17.10.2011

Hackensberger, A., Rappen für das Paradies. In: Die Welt 21.08.2013

Has the Arab spring failed? The Economist 13.07.2013

Hond, B. den., *Rode Lijn of niet, realist Obama denkt nog niet aan ingrijpen.* Trouw 23.08.2013

International Crisis Group., *Blurring the Borders: Syrian Spillover Risks for Turkey.* Europe report No. 225 30.04.2013

Irak kan terroristen niet meer aan, roep klinkt om inzet van drones. Friesdagblad 19.08.2013

Iran issues veiled military threat. In: World Net Daily 06.10.2011

Karadjis, M., *The Geopolitics of the Syrian uprising.* International Journal of Socialist Renewal. 13.08.2013

Kinzer, S., *Reset Middle East. Old Friends and new Alliances.* Saudi Arabia, Israël, Turkey, Iran. New York 2010

Koerkamp, G.G., *Poetin: VS liegen over gifgas, er zijn geen harde bewijzen.* Trouw 05.09.2013

Lawson, F.H., *Syria. Global Security Watch.* Trouw (2013)

Lesch, D.W., *Syria. The Fall of the House of Assad.* (2012)

Ludeker, I., *De strijdmacht van Assad verbrokkelt.* Trouw 13.08.2013

Ludeker, I., *Leger Egypte heeft even geen tijd voor de Sinaï.* Trouw 20.08.2013

Lucas, N., *Met gifgas win je de oorlog niet.* Trouw 23.08.2013

Marcus, A., *Blood and Belief. The PKK and the Kurdish fight for Independence.* New York 2007

Mühlmann, S., *Pakistans starker Mann vor Gericht*. In: Die Welt 21.08.2013

Pamuk, H./Solaker, G., *Turkey warns Syrian Kurds against 'dangerous' moves* 26.07.2013 (Reuters)

Pierik, P. (red), *Omwentelingen in het Midden-Oosten. Perceptie en gevolgen*. (Soesterberg 2012)

Report: *Jordan allows Israël to use its airspace for Syria attack*. Israel news 22.04.2013

Rodenbeck, M., *A Climate of Change*. The Economist 13.07.2013

Rössler, H-C., *Armee oder Anarchie*. In: Frankfurter Allgemeine Zeitung für Deutschland. 21.08.2013

Speetjes, P., *Kan Syrië zijn energie-ambities waarmaken?* In: Trouw 12.08.2013

Sullivan, A.O., *Syria's Alawites go on arms shopping spree*. In: Jerusalem Post 16.10.2011

Syria's Ramadan Massacre. 01.08.2011

Syrian and Kurds want Bashar Assad to stay. In: Pravda 12.10.2011

Syriën will sich 'mit allen Mitteln' verteidigen. In: Die Welt 27.08.2013

Uslu, E., *PKK-Syria axis?* In: Today's Zaman 09.10.2011

Uslu, H., *De rol van de vrouw in de Arabische Lente.* In: Perry Pierik (red.) Omwentelingen in het Midden-Oosten Soesterberg 2012

Uslu, H., *Turkije en de weg naar democratie.* (Soesterberg 2014).

Wilgenburg,W.van., *A New Syrian Identity for Kurds.* In: Rduaw 16.10.2013

http://www.gallup.com/video/162863/less-half-americans-closely-following-war-syria.aspx

http://www.gallup.com/poll/163112/americans-disapprove-decision-arm-syrian-rebels.aspx

http://www.gallup.com/poll/154997/Snapshot-NATO-Intervention-Libya-Unpopular-Arab-World.aspx

http://www.globalpolitician.com/default.asp?25397-turkey-antisemitism-jewish-Israël-terror/

http://www.kifkif.be/actua/maagdelijkheidscontroles-in-turkije

http://www.globalpolitician.com/default.asp?26932-wikileaks-turkey-usa-state-department

http://rt.com/news/syria-chemical-weapons-plot-532/